## About the Author

Someone who spends way too much time reading on their own, who should smile and speak more often, according to the family. I'm also really glad I can still walk and try to use my car less often, to stay on my feet more. Often listen to music, to keep my mind from wandering too far.

# A Cage within a Cage

**Mitch Mearns**

A Cage within a Cage

Olympia Publishers
*London*

www.olympiapublishers.com
OLYMPIA PAPERBACK EDITION

Copyright © Mitch Mearns 2023

The right of Mitch Mearns to be identified as author of
this work has been asserted in accordance with sections 77 and 78 of
the Copyright, Designs and Patents Act 1988.

**All Rights Reserved**

No reproduction, copy or transmission of this publication
may be made without written permission.
No paragraph of this publication may be reproduced,
copied or transmitted save with the written permission of the publisher,
or in accordance with the provisions
of the Copyright Act 1956 (as amended).

Any person who commits any unauthorised act in relation to
this publication may be liable to criminal
prosecution and civil claims for damage.

A CIP catalogue record for this title is
available from the British Library.

ISBN: 978-1-80439-441-0

This is a work of creative nonfiction. The events are portrayed to the best of the author's memory. While all the stories in this book are true, some names and identifying details have been changed to protect the privacy of the people involved.

First Published in 2023

Olympia Publishers
Tallis House
2 Tallis Street
London
EC4Y 0AB

Printed in Great Britain

## Dedication

To the ARI & Woodend Stroke East staff, who helped make an unbearable situation bearable. And to my parents, who did the same afterwards. Thank you.

# Prologue

When you think of a stroke, what springs to mind is an elderly person.

Or at least, much older than thirty.

It's a condition most believe only occurs to someone whose body is failing and aged. I suppose it's more accepted that a heart attack is possible in younger adults, but at the same time so are all the other subtle illnesses.

I still have no idea how it happened to me and I don't suppose I ever will, though perhaps medical knowledge will have advanced enough eventually, I'll likely be long gone.

For a few days prior I wasn't feeling so good: I had the worst flu symptoms such as light sensitivity, aches and pains, nausea, complete with vomiting, and a whole host of other joyful experiences. My personal hate is for the blocked or running nose, which I just find irritating and difficult to breathe easily with.

I never really get sick like that. I mean, I did, but only approximately once or twice a year, and usually only with much milder symptoms such as a sore throat and cough, maybe a blocked nose in one nostril that I needed to keep cleaning so as to not feel like my breathing was lopsided.

It seemed to be on and off, as for two days I was like this, then fine for a day, then bad again for another. That day was supposed to be a fine day, where I wasn't feeling bad at all. I had hoped it was all behind me – in the way you really wish to get better soon – but no such luck.

There wasn't anything that would lead me to even imagine what would happen to me next. Even if a stroke had been a possible option, like I said, most of us believe that it's something that can only happen to someone much older.

I look back every now and then, and still nothing sticks out in my memory. The most I can think of is that I had a stiff shoulder pain just before I got ill, but that was just bad posture I think for sitting at my home desktop for too long. Since when could 'bad posture' lead to this? If that truly were the case, then the video gaming industry was so screwed.

It didn't help at the time that if I even had felt something was wrong, we were in the middle of a global pandemic, so getting a hospital appointment to have anything checked was remote – unless you were willing to take a chance on catching it, since apparently according to the news it was much easier to get once there. The most I would have got was some kind of electronic consult on a tablet or computer, maybe even just a phone call. Those are all far too impersonal for me as I prefer face to face, where you can actually interact with someone as opposed to just a glass screen.

Maybe this'll be helpful to some, or maybe it won't. All I can say for sure is that… it happened to me, when the thought of it never once crossed my mind at the time.

# Chapter 1

It was when I came downstairs from the bathroom, halfway into the living room from the door to the sofa. Something in my head: a kind of wet splash from a single drop of cold water in the back-left of my head. Like the kind you feel when you're outside and it's just starting to rain on your skin, but only one drop this time, and it was inside my head and not on my hair or neck.

I stopped for a moment to more closely feel it, but there was nothing more that I could tell readily, just that something was wrong, yet I couldn't be more specific and half figured that it was nothing but me being paranoid. Rather than continue to stand in the middle of a room with a glass coffee table dangerously close by if I was going to have a fall, I moved a few steps and took a seat on the sofa, still feeling nothing but a sense of general unease.

I don't recall too much of that time, only that I started to feel worse in some way yet still couldn't determine how. That day of the week, I usually visited my grandmother at night, but I knew I wasn't up to it any more, and tried to call her on my nearby mobile phone.

It was weird though.

I'm right-handed and usually have full control of my fingers, but this time the result of what my brain was telling my hand to do wasn't what I wanted in practice.

There was no off-feeling in my head whilst moving the

limb, yet my finger couldn't press down on the correct buttons on the glass screen, or type anything by text. It was a jumbled mess that was getting steadily worse, and I began to have an inclination of what was happening. I tried speaking then, softly to myself, to confirm if what was happening to me was real, and not just some bad idea my paranoia had come up with.

I couldn't do it. What came out of my mouth sounded mumbled and echoed wrongly in my head, but of course my internal commentary was fine. It was at that point I realised my lack of fine finger control had spread slowly to my wrist now and I couldn't accurately move it. I just stupidly kept trying to use my phone to let my grandmother know I wouldn't be coming, with no success.

It was at around half-six in the evening when it happened, and I think it was around seven when I remember that my dad got up and went to bed – to watch something separate from me and my mom most likely in their room as he usually did. It was earlier than normal for him, as he normally stayed up until around half-seven when Emmerdale had finished.

I came round to my parents' most nights for food and company since I live alone, staying till late evening to watch crime dramas with my mom and keep her from falling asleep downstairs in a bad position on the sofa.

I don't know how much more time passed, only that it couldn't have been too long since it was still light outside. I also don't know what it was that alerted my mom that something was wrong with me, I just remember her saying we were going to the hospital, and that seemed to wake me up from my internal daze.

That was probably the time I admitted it to myself, as opposed to just a crazy thought of a condition that shouldn't have happened to someone in their thirties.

I was having a stroke.

I was still okay to get up at that point, but there was a lack of control starting from my right hand that kept spreading upward. Getting my shoes on with their laces was more challenging than I remember – ever tried to tie your shoe laces with just one hand? Your non-dominant one at that? I muddled through it, using my waning right hand as a static tool of sorts in the end.

I succeeded, after a few extra minutes more than usual through sheer force of will and personal annoyance, and then slipped on my coat that had all my things in it. I didn't like going anywhere without them: phone, money, keys etc. Especially since something could happen, and well, something really was happening, wasn't it?

I breathed a sigh of relief when I sat in the passenger seat of the car, knowing that I was moving (for now) in the right direction – towards the hospital. I remarked to myself we were in the middle of a pandemic and it was possible I'd catch COVID, but since the alternative was to die of a stroke, I figured I'd take my chances.

My parents didn't live too far from the local hospital, so we didn't have too long to wait to get there, only ten minutes or so. Whilst going there, I remembered a TV advert I'd seen a few times not long ago about being on the lookout for a stroke in a person. It was something like F.A.C.E or F.A.S.T, or maybe F.A.C.T.S as an acronym, can't remember what each letter stood for though.

It's different seeing it happen to someone else, and then experiencing it yourself; I assumed the victim would be feeling something, but the worrying thing was that I felt nothing. No pain at all, no burning or numb sensation to speak of. Just a slowly spreading inability to move half my body, subtly and sinisterly claiming more of me without warning.

The hospital looked slightly different when we rolled up, as it always did. As per any usual Scottish male under seventy, I eschewed any possible reason to see a doctor unless it was life threatening, so my visits were few and far between, emphasis on far. I still have no idea when that new multi-storey car park for visitors turned up, only now that there suddenly was one.

We didn't park there, however. We drove into a narrow area that still seemed partly under construction, to the small A&E entrance. I regretted my loss of legible speech then, as I'm pretty sure my mom parked in a disabled space and I wanted to say something about it, but considering the circumstance I kind of qualified.

My mom led me inside then like I was fragile, which was emasculating, but sadly necessary.

I had that strange mental feeling now that I was there, like all of this was actually real and I wasn't just going to blink and wake up in bed at home. She spoke for me at the front desk, and luckily seemed to have guessed what I assumed but couldn't say: that she suspected her son was having a stroke.

On TV, you see hospital documentaries depicting waiting areas of A&E being full of people, with bandages wrapped around the part of the body that had something wrong, some showing the tonal change from white to deep red. This particular one was all but empty though, just one other person that I could see calmly sitting waiting to be seen, no visible bandage in sight to give a hint to what was ailing him. All I can remember is that he wore a jacket, but the face is a blur.

At least I think it was a man.

# Chapter 2

Gender status aside, I didn't have to wait long to be seen. It was only about fifteen minutes I think, and I was seen before the person who was already there, maybe because what I had was more life threatening. I just kept on saying thank you to my mom for bringing me there, and continued to mentally regret that I couldn't use my phone to let my grandmother know that I wouldn't be round tonight.

When they did call for me, I was able to walk unsteadily with some support to the private room, or at least halfway. Of course, it was the one right at the end of a long hallway. I made it about halfway, then it was like my right leg just gave and I couldn't support my weight on it any more in an instant – if it hadn't been for my mom holding my arm at the time, I might've fallen down hard.

After that, the nurse went to get a wheelchair for me to sit in and be wheeled about so much faster than I had been walking previously, which gave me a sense of how bad things were now.

Whilst inside the nurse's room, we went through all the usual medical questions, whilst feeling a morbid sense of calm, but there was nothing wrong with anything said, I think. I was helped onto a movable bed early on when I went in, and luckily my mom was still around to do most of the answering. When I did have to talk, my voice was barely recognisable as my own, and I sometimes had to say things more than once and in shorter phrases to get the point across. I can't say for what it sounded like to others, but to me it was like a long tunnel echo, something you had to be focused on to pick up, and couldn't get the first time.

Of course, I had my internal commentary so I knew what I was saying, or wanted to anyway, but it was mildly annoying that my lips and mouth weren't exactly following my internal script all that clearly, and I kept having to make revisions part way due to a newly discovered verbal constraint.

There was lots of nodding from the person we saw, so I guess I somehow got my illegible point across. Either that or she didn't have the heart to ask me to repeat myself again for the third time.

She seemed to accept my mom's opinion of a stroke, and wheeled the bed I was on towards what I think was the triage area you tend to see on medical dramas. I forget the name, but instead of walls there were cubicle-sized areas of curtains to block your sight off, presumably so you don't see someone with a gushing red hosepipe where a limb should be.

Not much happened after I was given my own little curtain cubicle in the corner of the big room; I don't even know exactly how much time passed, but I think it was less than half an hour. I'd been taken through here on my own; my mom was left back at the office area near reception, who had been told they'd look after me. This area was for staff and patients only, I guess to keep the amount of foot traffic low.

Cue to me back on my own, clutching my jacket that

I'd taken off since it was too warm, yet it still had all my important things and I didn't want to accidentally leave it behind. I was still oddly calm, as if I was an observer listening to all the sounds around them but not able to affect things. Thank God I'd gone to the bathroom right before all of this happened, and hadn't had a chance to get a drink yet.

At some point later on, a nurse appeared in my area, but didn't really say anything to me other than a light hello, beginning to fill out some kind of form that was too far away for me to see; I'm guessing it was some kind of patient intake forms. They didn't need to ask me anything, and I hesitated to speak most of the time so as to not hear the echo in my voice, only saying short words most of the time. I'd just wave and smile like an idiot, and wonder when the hell I could get out of there, not knowing that this was just the start of a long-term visit that ended up spanning more than a week.

I wondered when I would see a doctor at that point, and someone seemed to hear me. It wasn't a real doctor in the end though, just a tablet on a stick that reminded me of an episode of *Big Bang Theory*. The one where Sheldon is too afraid to leave the apartment and remote controls what looks like a low budget version of Number Five from *Short Circuit* to be his stand-in.

Anyway, the doctor looked like she was in a bedroom, and I remember hoping I hadn't woken her up. She wasn't under the covers or anything, just sitting on the floor next to the bedside, I observed, but the nagging sense I had disturbed someone resting still stuck.

She asked a few questions, and I answered the best I could, basically about what had happened and how I ended up here. I narrated the circumstance as best as I could, describing the cold droplet feeling I remember feeling early on and my subsequent loss of control of my right side.

It wasn't easy to say more than a few words though, not because it was hard, but because I hated sounding like that, so I spoke slowly and simply, hoping not to be asked to repeat myself again too many times. I didn't have my mom around to act as translator any more, so I was forced to say more myself.

She concluded that it was most likely a stroke, and added that they were going to give me 'thrombolysis', some kind of blood clot dissolver. At that point, it hadn't been more than an hour or two since the symptoms, and it was still within the four and a half hour recommended window for giving it. Too much time after that and it would be less effective for the patient, causing the recovery process to be much longer.

It seemed to do the trick, since I don't think it spread any further after that, and I was glad I could still breathe with two lungs easily. I was still on the bed though, leaning up with a dead arm and leg weight were annoying, but I kept that to myself.

It was another wait then, with a blood sample taken after a cannular was added to my hand for steady fluids. I chose to have it on my left hand, the one I could still move. I didn't want to be reminded that my right arm and leg were now dead weight. Also didn't want to jerk or tug at it and cause damage to myself inadvertently.

I always hated needles, I mean it's not like I had an intense fear, I just really don't like the pain. It used to be called a small sting by the one about to do it, but I think now that it seems to have been changed at some point to a slight scratch. Picturing a scratch right before the pain hits somehow made it more tolerable.

Later I got an idea of the extent of the damage when I had to put on a gown and found out how difficult it was to undress in that situation, but at least I had privacy with the curtain around my area. I couldn't move my toes at all, nor my leg, and I had to concentrate and go slowly so as to not get angry at my body's inability to listen to my brain.

It wasn't long after that that I was moved again, this time away from the curtained cubicle and past a few others. No gushing hosepipes in sight, though I guess I would have noticed the pooling red puddle. I think one person held a bloody bandage to their head, but I can't be sure.

I laughed a little as I was wheeled around like a wide load on the bed, kind of liking that I didn't have to worry about the directions since I wasn't the driver for once. I was used to being the one driving, preferring the control to letting someone else have it.

I don't remember exactly where we went, anyone who's been in hospital knows it's like a maze designed to keep patients from escaping, though I sometimes wonder if they're meant to keep the staff and visitors in too.

After an elevator ride past the twisting hallways, we ended up in Ward three hundred and something: fifteen I think, or maybe thirteen. I was moved into a large room interspersed with beds, most of which were taken. There was one gap in the occupancies and I was moved there, in the middle of one of the sides, with beds at either side of me. The beds were more spaced apart now than they used to be, a few metres now I'd say, with a lockable cupboard and drawers to the side of them all to put your things in.

I could finally let go of the death grip I had on my jacket.

The room felt like it could have fit twelve beds, but that had been halved to six now with three on either long side.

Oh yeah, every other patient looked much older than me, by at least a few decades I'd guess.

## Chapter 3

It felt like when you were at a theme park, and you needed to be a certain height to go on the next ride. Kind of like 'you need to be this old to get in here'. There's always an exception to every rule, and I guess I was the current exception.

There were also a couple of private rooms at the far end, but I couldn't really move around to see anything up close, only that from the people going in, they were both occupied. From one of them I could hear the occasional groaning, an older female tone I guessed from the sound.

It was getting late then, after they moved me onto another bed, so I didn't have long to wait till lights out. This was January as well, so it had already got dark outside and the internal lighting gave a night-time feel. I guess I fell asleep at some point after that, since I don't remember much else. It was much earlier than when I usually fell asleep at around one a.m (don't judge), this time the lights went out at around nine to ten p.m.

I woke up the next day fairly early, probably since I went to sleep much earlier, maybe around six a.m. It was still dark all around, and fairly quiet. Hushed was the word I would use, and I endeavoured to try and remain quiet so as not to disturb the still-sleeping patients.

At that point I was faced with my biggest challenge of all: boredom.

There really is only so much time you can sleep and apart from meal times there wasn't anything else. Hospital visits had been cancelled since the pandemic to limit COVID spreading, so that wasn't something to look forward to. I normally like to read, but I only had my phone with me and didn't feel in the mood to be absorbed into an immersive story. I couldn't even really talk, so all I could do was look around myself, unable to even get up and walk and confined to my bed.

There was an option to be moved to an old-style padded chair, on the opposite side of the bed as the lockable cupboard. That was the extent of my movement options. There wasn't even the option to go the bathroom, just an oddly shaped cardboard bottle provided along with a pulling of the privacy curtains around your bed. Hardly private I felt, since everyone could more or less figure out what you were doing.

Thinking back, that really was a low point for me. I didn't need a bowel movement, luckily, so I avoided any messy issues that would have caused. I was also a neat freak about washing my hands, so the inability to do so disturbed me a little, but it's not like I touched a lot throughout the day due to my highly limited mobility.

There was some kind of touchpad screen that could play some TV channels, above the bed on a two or three-point tripod connected to the wall behind you, but I refused to pay hospital prices for a key-card to get them to play something watchable. Also, I couldn't just get up and get one from outside the room, where the dispenser was, and didn't want to hear myself ask someone for one.

A nearby patient did though, so I settled for listening to his as best I could and tried not to yawn too loudly. Easy enough to hide in the past, I just kept my mouth closed, but now my jaw seemed to want to yawn widely when the urge struck, and I didn't feel like tamping it down.

The day went by with not much to break down the time, apart from the meals and occasional bathroom moments. The room at the far end with the groaning woman had visitors at night, none of them dressed like hospital staff so I guessed they were relatives. I remember asking a nurse why she was allowed visitors, and her telling me that they didn't expect her to last through the night, and this was a chance for the relatives to have a last goodbye.

In the end, that did end up being her last day. I gather she had quietly slipped away in the night. I don't remember even seeing her once.

At some point, when I was sleeping, I figure they moved her body out on the bed, since I don't remember seeing anything. She was just gone, never to be seen again. That was the same room they moved me into just afterwards, and I recall feeling that it was a little uncaring, but deep down it didn't faze me and I knew that in a hospital, space had now become a premium, and I was just glad to get my own room and not be reminded so often of the age difference between me and the other patients.

I think that was the main reason for it, a nurse told me that they thought I would prefer a private room to myself as I was younger than everyone else.

It wasn't a unisex ward, as I don't remember seeing any other female patients, so perhaps she had been in there due to a lack of space elsewhere.

I hadn't thought far enough ahead; having my own room just meant that I had less to look at and barely anything to hear, making the boredom more obvious and less easy to ignore by people watching.

Beneath the gown I wore, I still had on my underwear, with some kind of diaper-water-absorber inside in case of 'accidents', to which I admit I had a few since I vaguely recall that my mind was in a dull haze, still cognisant yet wallowing in my condition rather than my normal thinking ahead. Again, no bowel movements though, which ended up being a blessing. I'm not sure I would have been able to live it down being changed like that at my age, no matter how much I needed help. It was something private and always should be as far as I was concerned.

I'd end up ignoring the wet feel until it was time for a clothing change, not wanting to bother the staff any more than I had to and just prayed that I had enough dry spares.

Now that I had my own room, I found it also came with an attached bathroom, and that instead of a cardboard bottle to relieve myself, I just had to call on the nearby bedroom buzzer to the nurse and they would take me. It wasn't far, but it gave me a chance for a few minutes to interact with other people, to know that life existed beyond the door.

It wasn't all manual though; they had some kind of metal Zimmer with a few extras on coasters. There was a platform you put your feet on, a vertical padded bit to lean your knees against, and a waist high bar with handles you could hold onto to stay upright. There was a bit at the back that you could sit on when they locked it in, making it comfortable enough to move. It was good to see things at my usual height again, and not be locked into a lower position of perspective.

I still don't remember what it was called, but it helped a lot.

But like I said, I didn't want to be a bother, so I endured the wetness when I couldn't hold it in any longer, holding it in as long as I could and feeling a release when I couldn't, despite knowing what it was and how it felt.

There was one night I remember though, after the lights were all out. One of the other patients in the multi-room right outside mine had wandered in and was looking out the window. I think his name was Colin, and he was nice enough. He was in his fifties I'd guess, and was now able to walk about steadily, but I think his stroke affected his cognitive functions in some way, as he seemed slower to grasp things and respond.

We didn't talk really, I just held up the nurse's button and tried to ask if he wanted help, but he shook his head and went back to looking outside. It had snowed a day or two before, so, despite the dark, it wasn't completely black outside where the streetlights didn't touch.

He didn't say anything after that and I didn't see a problem letting him continue to enjoy the view. He left not long afterwards, only having stayed for a few minutes, and I envied his ability to walk in and out of a room when he wanted. When would I be able to do the same? There was no alternative in my mind, I would get better in time, the only question was how much.

I was lucky later on, it seemed they allowed one visitor per person so I got to see my mom a few days later for a little while. That was the point I realised I had another symptom; when I talked, I'd get far too emotional with things in general, and wouldn't be able to stop myself from crying or laughing, despite that I didn't feel so much that way in my head, and hated that I couldn't keep things in like I was used to, that my lack of control was so evident, my sense of weakness so obvious to others.

I'm not one for talking much or long conversations, but I was honestly so bored that I was glad for the distraction from the white walls I'd stared at till then. She brought in a few things for me, some fresh clothes and basics that reminded me I hadn't brushed my teeth or shaved in a day or two, and still didn't want to try it with my left hand alone. I'd probably slice my neck open by accident with the razor or nearly choke somehow on the toothbrush.

She said she'd also take in my work laptop and personal hard drive, which had a few things on it I could watch; but that would take till the next day or until I next saw her. The visit wasn't long, but I felt better after seeing someone I knew, but was still left alone in that room at the end of it after a short period of time.

I think the nurses felt sorry for me, since one of them offered a sort of compact DVD player/mini screen and a few DVDs to keep me busy. The choice was rather limited though, I think I only had a choice of four films and ended up going with just one; *Meet the Parents* with Ben Stiller and Robert DeNiro, mostly because it was a comedy and I needed a laugh.

Things seemed to pass quicker after that until the next day when my mom turned up again to see me. I realised I'd forgotten to mention about my personal hard drive with all my media on it, and only mentioned the laptop without any material, mentally hitting myself. She did bring in my tablet, but the books I read are web novels on the internet, and I didn't think I'd have access. I could've used my phone as a hotspot, but I didn't want to do anything I probably shouldn't, what with the medical equipment around. That and with nothing else to do, I'd end up eating away at my monthly data in less than a day.

At least I still had the mini-DVD player.

What came after was a day where I watched *Meet the Parents* three or four times in a row, since I didn't fancy any of the other films, and honestly can't remember what they were.

# Chapter 4

The next day my mom took in the hard drive so I was no longer bound to the film like some sort of entertainment junkie in constant need of a fix. Any more and I'd have started repeating their lines in sync internally, since I almost knew it word for word by this point.

Since it was a comedy, I also couldn't help but laugh at moments, found that my lack of emotional control also extended to when I was happy as well as sad. Since it was a private room, no one else got to see my lack of control, but I still knew and needed to keep myself distracted from the monotony.

What was my choice once I had one? Disney movies!

I watched them a lot growing up, and they're a part of me at this point, and I occasionally watch one at times at random. Theres no complicated plot, no intricate twist at some point, just a classic fairy tale to enjoy and stop thinking to. The reason something is a cliché is because it works.

My first unoriginal choice was also the first movie: *Snow White and the Seven Dwarves*. I hadn't seen it in years and felt like seeing it now.

I watched a few more to fill the time, mostly my favourites that I hadn't seen for ages. *Sleeping Beauty*, *Hercules* and *Emperor's New Groove* were the list. The story and soundtrack of *Hercules* is one of the best, and I still couldn't help but let myself cry or laugh at the emotional points. I love all of the music in that one, and even listen to all of it until the end of the credits.

In between my entertainment crisis, I forgot to mention that there were a few doctors making their rounds. Nothing specific, at least for me, just a check to that I see I wasn't any worse off and that the drugs they'd given me seemed to be working. There was also a point where I was taken away for an MRI/brain scan to see what was going on inside my head, or at least what had happened.

There was some kind of dye they injected in me that burned a little as it travelled through my veins and made parts of my head feel warm until it cooled. I felt it as it travelled up my arm to my head. Nothing painful, but I could feel it. The first scan didn't seem to work well, however, since they injected me with more dye and I got that hot feeling again.

What they saw, I don't remember getting to see, but I think it confirmed I had a stroke somehow and where in the brain, though I wouldn't know the details of it all until a while later.

It was an eventful moment in one where there was literally nothing else to do but lay in bed or sit in the sofa all day, watching a few things on the laptop, so I was glad for the distraction.

During the doctors' occasional rounds, one of them also tested my sense of feeling in my feet, poking one of them and asking me to tell which one he touched when my eyes were closed. I could easily tell, since although I couldn't move anything on my right side, I still had perfect feeling and sensation.

At this point, I didn't know if I was going to get any better, so still being able to feel something was better than nothing. It's strange, I still felt nothing was wrong mentally, without pain or discomfort. It's just that the connection to my right leg, arm and mouth didn't seem to perfectly connect with what I was imagining, like something had gone wrong part way.

I was moved again about half a week in, this time to the front of the ward right before the main entrance, with more glass at the upper wall areas instead of plaster panels, to let in more light I'd guess. Problem was, they were higher than I could sit up, so they might as well not have been there, but at least it was brighter overall.

Not much really happened after that, I had my media on my laptop to keep me busy, since I still didn't want to read, so I was finally able to distract myself from watching an empty room. Meal times and bathroom breaks were still the only way to break down the time, as well as the once-per-day visit from my mom with her daily update of what had happened outside.

I do remember the staff being really nice though, and I didn't like to bother them since there were others in the ward who were likely worse than me. A fairly safe bet, I believe, since I was the youngest there by decades.

It was in the middle of a pandemic too, and every time you saw someone, their faces were covered in a face mask with a visor over it, their hands gloved, and a plastic apron over their front. Most of which they had to dispose of every time they came out of my room and get a new set. I recall seeing a bin full of the stuff at one point, and the idea of so much thrown away stung my miserly tendencies.

After about a week, I was told that I was being moved to a different building; some kind of specialised stroke building/unit rather than a ward in a massive hospital. Since it was a change of scenery, I didn't complain, not that I easily could anyway. So far, there hadn't been any improvement in me that I could tell with the level of control I had, nor with my voice, but it had only been less than a week. Turns out my limbs did move, albeit very, very slowly, and only with the constant intent to move something after about a minute would I see the virtual translated into physical, like some slow-motion replay.

I checked and double checked that I had it all packed and ready, not that there was much. What I did have though, I didn't want to lose: laptop, keys, phone, hard drive, jacket, bag, clothes etc.

I waved goodbye to the nurses as I left, imagining their smiles behind those masks. One jokingly said not to forgot them, a hard request really, what with all the masks on, I found it difficult to differentiate between people.

I haven't forgotten their kindness in dealing with me, especially in such a trying time; when physically touching a stranger with your bare hands came with a potential death sentence, they still helped me, and I'm grateful for that.

Although it's been over a year, I still can't recall the ward number exactly, to go back and say thank you in person. The effects of the pandemic are still being felt too in our health service, so I don't want to end up going in as a visitor, and wind up staying as a patient again, assuming I'm even allowed to go in when there isn't a patient I'm visiting. No offence, but everyone who's ever been stuck in hospital for a while knows this feeling: of just wanting to get out and stay out.

I think that trauma is partly to blame for everyone keeping bad symptoms to themselves, refusing to go to the doctor until you cough up a lung or two.

Back to me: There was finally some new mental stimulus for me as I was sat in a wheelchair with my bags, moved out by a porter with my few belongings, all of which I clutched tightly, as if someone was going to pilfer them when I wasn't ready.

I think at that point I really needed to get out of there.

We navigated our way through the maze-like interior, down elevators and corridors to the eastern exit – where I could finally breathe some fresh air after a week long. It's not just that the scenery is the same inside: no windows are opened and no wind or breeze exists. It's warm, yes, but your mind needs the stimulation that a sense of hot and then cold provide, or else you feel yourself going slightly mad due to a form of prolonged sensory deprivation.

I took a deep breath in when I was outside, letting it out slowly and knowing that this was a step (or a drive) in the right direction.

# Chapter 5

The car was one of those van types for rear wheelchair access, with a pull-down ramp at the back instead of a boot. I think there might have been a logo on the outside, but can't remember. I was usually the one that drove others around, so it was a rare novelty that I would be the one to get driven about here.

I couldn't stop looking at the scenery as we went past the hospital grounds, still finding traces of snow along the curbs. There hadn't been much this year, and it hadn't lasted, thank God, for the sake of all motorists!

It was colder outside, but not unbearably so, I was fine just wearing my jacket. Not enough to discount the freedom I felt when I sucked in a cold breath anyway. Plus, I was all wrapped up in my normal clothes, not like I was still in a hospital gown or pyjama shorts.

The trip was only a few miles, and didn't end up lasting that long until we pulled up to my new temporary home. It was close to my parents' too, so much that they could walk there easily rather than drive and park nearby. It wasn't till shortly after that I learned that the building was considered a bubble for patients, and that no visitors were allowed inside at all, apart from staff.

The building was more long than tall, with about two floors. The entrance was on the right on a long side, just next to a small car park. The patient rooms were all on the left side, further down the hall.

I was wheeled into an open room with three other residents at about the middle of the hall on the left of it as you go down; all of those already in there looked much older than me. You know, despite me being told that having a stroke at thirty was only 'uncommon' and not too rare, the fact that I was clearly the youngest patient I could see in the building, by a few decades, made me think otherwise.

The room could clearly fit six – judging by the wardrobes and drawer sets I saw – but they had removed the middle bed from each side of the room to accord with two-meter distancing. The whole place was more homely than a sterile white hospital, with wood panelling in places and overall giving a feel of an older décor. It wasn't terrible though, and made me feel more comfortable.

There was a communal TV at the far end, right in front of the large half-height windows that spanned the back wall, leading outside to the car park. There were only the basic Freeview channels I believe, but it was only ever left on BBC One, usually with a low volume so as not to let the sounds leave the room. I was in charge of the remote most of the time, but I just left the same channel running that they were all used to, only watching occasionally.

I still had my laptop and media drive, so there were other things I could watch privately if I wanted, whereas they seemed to have already chosen in silent debate that BBC One was going to be left running.

Imagine a square for the layout: I was in the lower left point next to the entrance, whereas all my roommates had the other three. From the top left working clockwise, there was

Tarlock, which we thought was too complicated and unusual, so we called him T. The name made me think of a character from an old TV series, though our version wore a lot less gold and was much milder in temperament.

He was in his early sixties, I think, though I never got a clear age on any of them. The type that is still fairly active, I'd say, in that point of semi-retirement where he still felt he needed to keep himself busy. His case was the opposite of mine, where he lost the control of his left side instead, but unlike me he didn't have much feeling or sense of touch left in the limbs.

His case was further along by a month or two, but you could tell that he was getting better and would eventually be let out. There was also an air of cheeriness around him, of calm that I appreciated. He wasn't too talkative, but responded when he was mentioned, occasionally coming out with a few ironic remarks that made me laugh.

In the top right was the problem child of the room, in so much that you can call a man over seventy a child. I suppose if you've even seen or read Benjamin Button, you get the idea.

His name was George, and his case was one of the worse ones. Both of his legs were wrapped in bandages, broken I think but I'm not sure what happened exactly. One of them I think he injured not long ago, but I've no idea how. He also had on a diaper and needed changing multiple times a day, for everything that entailed.

To make matters worse he could barely talk, similar to me, but worse: you needed to concentrate on the sounds and syllables he was saying and let your mind wander to come up with the words, and even then, you didn't always get it right. He usually gave up after you failed to get what he was saying a few times, a frustrated feeling clear in his posture.

Same as me, his stroke affected his right side too, and his current condition haunted me for a while, as if he was a living example of what I may end up as, or what I had to eventually look forward to.

The last person at the lower right of the square formation was William, who preferred to be called Rich. I'd guess he was in his fifties, closer to me in age than any of the others, and the chatty one of the bunch. His left side had gone, yet his outgoing nature hadn't. He kept my spirits up a lot, spoke a lot about his family and especially his young granddaughter. You could tell he really loved her, and I knew he was a decent – if boisterous – person.

He had a dog too, well he said it was a dog when he showed me the photo. Looked more like a bear to me – Bailey I think he called her. It was another point in his favour, as anyone who has and cares for a dog is all right with me.

Through our one-sided conversations, I got small hints into his life: He was a carer for his wife, who oddly enough had previously had a stroke some years ago and was wheelchair bound. In his case it was possibly the build-up of stress that caused his stroke, but I never knew much about the others to compare stories. His stroke happened at an unlucky time too, while he was out shopping with his wife; he just fell forward right through a glass table when it happened, but luckily the only thing that broke was the glass.

Once again, I was glad that I'd sat down when I felt something was wrong, or else that glass table in my parents' living room could have shared the same fate, a few shards possibly causing some other damage in the process.

Anyone who is an introvert would understand how much his talking at times out of nowhere annoyed me, or his too loud phone calls he made to his wife, where I could easily hear the other side of the call from across the room. I wasn't stupid though, and creating any kind of issue with people I had no choice but to share a room with wasn't smart. Especially when I couldn't really move around much.

Honestly, I think I'm just too used to being alone and seem to prefer it at times.

Even so, I still grinned and nodded in all the right places, but still couldn't respond in much more than just simple words that retained that echoing sound in my head. I could have recorded what I sounded like on my phone and played it back, but I didn't want to know, it felt like doing that would make things more real, less something that I could play off as a part of my vivid imagination.

Same with my face. There were no mirrors there, or many reflective surfaces really – probably on purpose – and I didn't want to take a picture of my lopsided face, only to end up upset at the result. The only thing knowing for certain would do was make me feel worse, so better to live in ignorance.

# Chapter 6

The meal times were the same as the hospital, if only a little later. They got the meals from there, presumably from the same kitchen, and after serving everyone else someone drove them over. It wasn't too far from us, but some things did end up drier as a result, but it was all still fine.

Soup was offered with every lunch as an appetiser, and I always had it. For evening dinner times there was a main and dessert, one or two times a nurse was nice enough to give me two desserts if there was one spare. I only really felt full after I had an extra serving, but I didn't want to take too much. What we were getting was already a measured serving, although who knows how they actually measured the diet of each person. The portions were on the small/medium size, which I reckon is all most older people can eat nowadays. It reminded me of my mom, who had an appetite like a sparrow.

I don't think I mentioned this, but eating with your left hand is hard – especially as a right-handed person. It felt strange and wrong, but the annoyance and frustration were quickly overridden by my hunger and need to eat. Rice dishes were the hardest, yet with enough time and motivation I think you can teach yourself almost anything. I never resorted to using my bare hand – that would have been cheating – and I could be more creative than that, moving the food to the side of the plate and sucking it off with my mouth. Well, at least I didn't use my hands, even if I probably looked like a bit of a savage.

We all had our own special wheelchairs too, each fitted simply and ergonomically for our needs. In my case, there was a padded brace for my right arm, with a soft paddle area where I could rest my hand on the armrest. I remember one time they accidentally swapped mine and Rich's chairs, but both of us realised it soon enough and swapped back after the nurses wiped them down for us.

It was a Tuesday when I was moved there, and not much else happened throughout the week. I got a visit from the resident consultant, a Doctor Cozins, who video-called my parents in too, since they couldn't be there in person as per usual. I found out later that my parents needed my brother's help to set it up, who had been out of the shot. I guess the older generation would always be a little technologically illiterate.

It was just going over my case, things I already knew since I lived with the symptoms he was describing, and ended with putting me on the physiotherapy rotation schedule they had for the following week. Nothing much, as their usual patients were much older; just one to test my legs, one for my hand and arm movement, and one for my speech.

To break down the day, I'd created a sort of bathroom schedule for myself. Ever since I came there and noticed George's condition, I refused to have any more wet accidents, especially with more witnesses in the room. The atmosphere was more homely too, less clinical, and I didn't want to ruin that. Still hadn't had a bowel movement either, in over a week now, and I was being given some laxative tablets now too as well as the blood thinning medication at night.

The medication I was on was one tablet a day of 80mg Atorvastatin, which was big and oval like. I'd say about 15mm along the long edge, but I never had any issue with swallowing them along with a glass of water, always showing my empty mouth to the nurse to confirm I'd swallowed it. Some patients didn't like to, George being one of them. He always grumbled unhappily when it was time for it, being given liquid form mostly, since that was an option over the tablets.

Since I needed to call for help to be wheeled to the bathroom, I tried to do it as little as possible, so as not to be a problem. They had their own lifting Zimmer-like frame, same as the hospital used.

I could've moved myself to the room at the back with a little effort, but I was told that I needed to let them do it for me, something about safety concerns. I was too used to doing things myself, and needing to call for help every time you wanted to go to the bathroom was pretty degrading, I thought, but I could only suck up my frustrations.

I went to the bathroom once after each meal, and once late at night before I went to bed and lights went off. That ended up being around nine p.m for us, and closer to ten for the rest of the rooms since they were further down the hall and we were first in line. I was used to going to sleep much later (around one a.m in the morning) so I often found myself wide awake and staring into space. Usually, the curtains around each bed were pulled out to give everyone privacy as they slept, but it didn't do anything for the sounds, which you picked up on much easier in the dark.

Luckily none of the others snored in the end, don't believe anyone mentioned I did either.

The following day came, and as always you don't realise when you exactly fell asleep, only that it was like you blinked and the night passed. At least your mind doesn't feel as tired or heavy as it did a second ago.

With another day came another set of challenges. The first one: getting dressed by myself.

It's really not easy when half of you is dead weight. This wasn't hospital attire either, this was putting on my normal clothes. After wriggling around behind the curtains, I managed to slip on my clothes without help, but then came the hard part.

Socks.

When I had left the main hospital, I had help getting into my things, and taking them all off the previous night had been so much easier, even one armed. Like then, I could have received help if I wanted, but I saw this as a challenge, and if I was like this for the rest of my life then I needed to learn to do this by myself as soon as possible.

It was still maybe too early for that kind of thinking, but I wanted to take back some form of control. Being able to dress myself, instead of sitting about all blank-like, waiting for someone to acknowledge my existence and help, didn't appeal to me in any way.

Now, back to the socks.

You probably don't realise how much you move your foot to make it easier to slip on your socks, and in that moment, I almost shouted in anger. The trick was to pack it together and roll it over your foot, as opposed to the normal way I was used to of just slipping it in.

Altogether it took me over thirty minutes the first time to get fully presentable, a far cry from my previous dress up moments of less than a minute.

I'd done it though, and laid back in my wheelchair in relief when it was over, admittedly feeling a little proud of myself.

# Chapter 7

Then there was breakfast not long after, normally simple cereal with milk and fruit juice, followed by some toast and tea or coffee. The medication I was on prevented me from ever having grapefruit juice again, and I didn't like the unoriginal orange or apple juice choice, so I just went for whatever unusual flavour they had at the time. Passion fruit juice was normally the option I went with.

After that, I realised that I hadn't brushed my teeth in a while – after a nurse asked us all if we wanted to – and finally felt up to giving it a try. I was given a little bowl of warm water and some towels, likely to make up for any spills. It was like eating, a new learning curve I had to get used to by brushing with my left hand instead of my right. The trick was to not rush and take my time, and after five minutes or so I was happy enough with the fresh feel in my mouth, and the bits of cereal no longer stuck between my teeth. Moving my head in time with my hand also helped.

There wasn't anything else to do apart from amuse yourself between meals. During the following week, I had my physiotherapy classes, but on the weekends, there was nothing to do but stay in your room. Most days were the same too.

At least there was a shower there that I could use.

Each morning you could choose to wash yourself with a warm wet cloth and basin, or have a shower on a plastic chair. I choose to alternate between days to keep things different, enduring the challenge of showering myself like that and getting dried on my own.

To break it down; I woke up early around six or seven, the lights were put on by the morning staff when they changed shifts with the night one at around eight, followed by a toilet visit, cleaning myself and changing, breakfast at nine, and teeth done shortly after. Then lunch at twelve, another bathroom break, then dinner at five with another toilet visit.

Finally at around nine at night, when everyone else seemed to have silently decided to go to bed, I made one last trip to the bathroom before getting back to bed and changing into my pyjamas, ready to stare blankly at things until at some point I managed to lose consciousness.

A rather dull day really, especially when you consider that I'd more or less be in the same room all day, aside from the attached bathroom and shower visit if I chose it. Oh yeah, the TV was put on at nine, and switched off at the same time in the evening, always on the same channel (BBC One).

At some point during the day, I'd started to read again on my tablet, and I'd always been good at letting myself be absorbed in a good story, so I never really felt too bored. It was the lack of being able to do anything else that annoyed me, or that I needed to call for help when I knew it wouldn't be too hard to get into the bathroom myself unaided.

That was what stung the most.

For books, I'd started reading web novels a year or so prior, so when I got the building's Wi-Fi password, getting access to the internet for that wasn't an issue. In the evening, after dinner, I would stop reading and get out my laptop to watch something, sometimes a Disney, sometimes an old British sitcom to give me a good laugh or two. I'd still have outbursts of laughs at times, but they were happening less now, maybe because I had an audience and didn't want to call attention to myself.

I had headphones though, so it wasn't like I disturbed their television time.

Visits weren't allowed in person, but my parents came round a few times and I got to see them through the room window at the back, for all the privacy that gave. To hear them, they called me on my phone and I tried to speak as clearly as I could.

To me, I still sounded like echoed crap, not sure what they heard but whatever. They seemed to respond to what I said after a second or two, so it was clear I was still understandable if you listened hard enough, which you could tell even over the phone that they were doing. Once or twice they even took the family dog round, so I got to see her too through the window as they were lifted up to see me.

Big surprise, I'd break down in tears often and sound even worse. It was like there was more pressure on my head when I got too emotional, which made it harder for the words to come out less slurred and mumbled.

Sometimes they'd just phone me when they couldn't make it up in person, and I'd still be a mess at times. I spoke in a loud way, trying to force the correct vowel sounds out with more volume, so everyone in the room could easily hear me, and how emotional I got. Rich kept telling me it was okay, and to just let it all out but that was difficult for me as I always kept things in. At least I didn't feel as embarrassed any more after what he said.

He was just as bad on the phone to his wife, for which my hearing could easily pick up both sides of the conversation. He was on his phone often, sometimes using Facetime and sometimes just the phone. He broke down a few times, sounding less like his usual self. All I could do was look as if I wasn't hearing it, trying not to intrude on such a private moment.

There was no real privacy at all, but when you had little to do through the day, anything came as an interesting distraction that your mind latched onto.

The first full week after the weekend had my first scheduled physiotherapy sessions: The first one was for legs, for which they rolled me into a different room with some simple gym-like equipment. I think I had two sessions of that my first week, on separate days.

I can't recall if it was the first or second week, but at some point, they got me back on my feet, just to stand and not walk, which was a massive leap forward from when I was bedridden all day. It was at that point when I realised that I was actually going to get better, that I was getting better over time and would be able to walk again soon, rather than stuck in the state of needing help for everything.

I freely admit that I cried then for a few seconds when the thought hit me, I don't think I'd admitted to myself how hard that would have been for me until I felt the relief of knowing it wouldn't happen.

Aside from that there was a large rubber ball that I

needed to roll my right leg over, a few other simple things like school cones and props to get me to do easy partial movements with my hip and leg. You probably don't realise the motion you go through to walk, or just how many muscles are involved, with every moving part of your lower body coming together for just one motion.

The reason I fell at the start while walking into A&E was because the stroke had taken my sense of balance too, so I wasn't able to feel comfortable supporting my weight through my hip and core, kind of like I'd forgotten how to walk due to loss of local muscle memory.

They had a sort of cycling machine too, where you could stay in your wheelchair and put your feet on the pedals, whereupon the machine would rotate the pedals themselves automatically and you could feel like your legs were making that walking motion.

Each session lasted about an hour, and it wasn't far to go either as it was just a few rooms down the hall in the same building. The trip there and back gave me more of a glimpse into my surroundings beyond just what that multi-room had. It was only the ground floor, but I gather that things must've been similar on the first. There was a staircase and elevator upward, but I couldn't say how many floors the building had, it wasn't something I paid attention to as I came in.

I do know that the building I was in was called Stroke East and that there was an opposing west building, but I don't believe there was a north or south.

# Chapter 8

The other session I had was for my hand and arm.

I only had about one of those per week, and it was to do simple exercises, like running it along different textures. It was the kind of class that gave you homework too, green putty the size of a tennis ball with a charming name (sputum) to be exact.

There was a sheet of A4 paper with some different finger movements to make with your affected hand while using it, like pulling, pressing or shaping. I used it a few times a day to give me something to do, feeling like I could move my hand and fingers more and more with each day that passed. The progress was slow, but eventually I could see the change in me daily.

At first, I had thought that my right side didn't receive any signals from my brain, but not long later, as I started to get better, I realised that I still was, albeit that the signal was being translated into movement very, very slowly. I even sort of timed it in my boredom.

If normally it takes less than a second for you to think of the action 'curl finger' for example, or something else like that, then the time for me had been extended up to almost a minute from start to finish, where I also had to constantly think about the action I was doing. It wasn't hard or painful, but the annoyance in me built with the lack of instant movement we all take for granted.

Luckily, that time for me seemed to be shortening by a

little bit a day, evident by my exercise performance, that the nurses kept having to make harder for me. They also remarked that I was getting better pretty quickly, and said that it must have been due to my younger brain. I remember one of them saying that they wish they'd recorded it to show me how far along I was coming in just a few weeks, but I don't think anyone expected me to get better that fast.

As for me, I knew from the moment that I stood up again that I was going to recover back to normal, the timeframe didn't really matter to me so much at that point.

I do remember the consultant saying that to get better in under six months was good, and taking up to a year was normal. Anything after that and you'd have to live with the results, but I didn't reckon that it would take me that long at the rate I was going. He did mention that some could recover fast, in three months, so that was what I aimed for in my mind, and my recovery pace didn't seem far off that.

The final session of the week was known as speech therapy. That one felt more private, where I and a nurse were in a much smaller admin-type room, practicing different word and vowel sounds. The nurse was young I think, and I can't apologise enough for the way I minced and mumbled my words in places. She was so nice, and patiently listened to me to work out what I was saying, allowing me to feel more comfortable speaking like that in front of someone.

I still wish I had been able to see her face to see her expression, to be able to tell that she was getting what I said, instead of just assuming it.

I remember thinking that it was fine if I always talked like that and she was the one who gave me the confidence to think that way. When you can't properly talk, just having someone there willing to listen and able to understand you makes so much of a difference. Family and friends are different, it's the contact with strangers that helps.

There was another nurse too, one that Rich seemed to enjoy teasing and getting teased back by. Was Brenda her name? Or was it Glenda? Anyway, she told me she had been in a bad motorcycle accident, ending up in hospital herself in the past. She knew what it was like to be trapped inside yourself at a hospital, and told me that it wouldn't be long until I was back on my feet thanks to all my rapid progress.

I eventually did have a bowel movement, by the way, but don't worry I won't describe it, although they do ask you to, funny enough. They even have an image chart and everything that you can point to if you don't want to say. I really didn't like taking the laxatives, and after that I didn't have to. The idea of also being dependant on medication as well as other people to go to the bathroom wasn't such a good one.

Personally, I think my body just wasn't used to these new stimulus and locations, so it took a while for it to calm down.

I'll admit, at first, I really wanted to get out of there. The place felt more and more like an elderly care home that I'd been mistakenly locked up in, and I wanted home, to somewhere more familiar to me. I even asked my parents over one of our phone calls to push for me to get out, in my own version of barely understandable English of course.

I knew I was being unreasonable now, they even said I was lucky to get a place there and not still be in the main hospital. All I can say is that my mind wasn't calm early on. I was in an unusual place, with a bad condition, and I was continually told that I would be able to leave 'eventually'. I swear, that's one of the worst things you can hear from a doctor: it'll get better when it gets better. It's basically a verbal shrug, and completely undermines their position in your head as someone who actually knows what they're doing.

Thinking back now, it really was the best place for me. Nothing would have really changed if I had been at home, just that I would have put more strain on my parents, letting them see me like that. Where I was, I could receive physiotherapy and care, not forgetting the current pandemic which meant we were in a sort of bubble.

Hard to believe nearly a year on and we were no further from lockdown, especially with BBC One news sensationalising the problem. I mean, didn't they have something else to report on instead of constantly mentioning that? If you're sick or ill, you shouldn't watch the news – it'll only depress you more.

After a week or so, I'd calmed down, and more or less accepted that I would be stuck there until I could walk out. I later learned that my neighbour George had been there for over six months, and I internally shuddered at the idea of being here all that time. I know I'm a homebody, but that sounded more like a prison sentence, especially with the near constant care he was needing, and I promised myself that I wouldn't be in that position for at least half of that time.

Rich and 'T' had only been there for a month or so longer than me, with the latter seeming to be on the road to recovery. Rich seemed no different from me, aside from his speech being more or less clear sounding, despite the length of his stay. I worried for him, but I didn't really have the space to be worried about anyone other than myself at that moment, but I hope he's doing better now.

I can't for the life of me remember the names of all the

nurses that helped me, especially when they always wore medical face masks to make putting a name to a face that much harder.

Brenda/Glenda is the only one I can recall, mostly because Rich teased her a lot and she was really nice.

At one point she mentioned some recent news online, about someone else of a similar age to me who'd also had a stroke in the city. Comparatively, it was scarily similar to my own case, and I realised how lucky I had been in the grand scheme of things.

He was thirty-eight, and living alone like me. When his stroke came, he was alone at home and it took three days for someone to come round and notice. The quicker you get the medication needed to combat a stroke, the better, and in his case, it would take a long time for a recovery, if any was even possible.

The day I had a stroke, I had been alone almost the entire time. I was working at my office place on my own, having seen not a person all day due to work from home restrictions at the time. The first people I had seen since the sun rose were my parents in the evening, who I had come round to visit, and just half an hour after I had arrived, it happened.

I think that was what really helped calm me down, that my luck had been decent enough to mitigate what was a life-threatening event into more of a temporary inconvenience.

It could have been so much worse.

# Chapter 9

The scheduling of my time helped, despite how lame it sounds to revolve your life around a bathroom and eating schedule. It helped keep me sane, to have a routine, I believe, and I would advise everyone else to do the same when facing a strange and prolonged circumstance in an unusual place such as this.

There was only one minor incident that I had whilst there, and nothing came of it apart from slightly dented pride. In short, my wheelchair fell over... with me still in it unfortunately.

My own fault really.

If you ever use a wheelchair of your own, and it has brakes on the back wheels, always put both of them on at once or none at all. For me, I had stupidly thought that one would be enough, allowing me to pivot on it with my legs on the ground, as a means of getting rid of some nervous energy in a fidgety sort of way. You know the kind, like tapping or swinging a limb.

Think I must've overcorrected or pushed too far, as I tipped over on my right side at one point and landed hard on the solid floor. As luck would have it, the chair seemed to absorb most of the impact without any damage, not even giving me a bruise, aside from to my pride. Although I couldn't get back up myself the nurses said, even though I wanted to try. In typical health and safety fashion, the nurses said they had to do it for me, and make sure I was okay, including document the whole incident.

Bloody paperwork.

The whole world revolves around some of the most tedious things, not as if someone was ever really going to read about it all.

Nothing had been around me when I fell over, fortunately too, so that was another crisis somehow averted: didn't even make a mess with my water.

Once a week the cleaning staff came round too, giving the room a good clean over. I can't remember if they only changed the bed sheets once a day, or once a week, but I think the latter. The curtains that could wrap around each bed were also replaced if they'd been used, though from what they were saying, I gather that they were starting to run out.

Aside from meal times, there was also someone who came around every two hours or so asking if you wanted tea or coffee, sometimes even giving you some biscuits if it was mid-day. Liquids are important to stay hydrated, I understood, and so never ended up turning down a cup that was offered to me.

My aunt had also sent me a care package of sorts: a little bag with some packets of sweets, sports drinks and a gaming magazine to give me something to read. That really helped, and I think reading that magazine helped me want to get back to reading in the first place.

I wouldn't say that I had much trouble sleeping, more that I was having trouble adjusting to the different bedtime for me. I have no idea how long it took me to nod off, just that I felt fine when I woke up, not drowsy and half-asleep as you normally get when you wake up at home, but instantly alert.

It was probably the new location filling me with a sense of anxiousness, knowing that I wasn't at home and unable to act like I was completely safe. It wasn't fear or anything bad, nor did it seem to fill me with much sense of stress. Just a knowing that I couldn't afford to be as lazy as usual, I guess.

I think it was near the end of the second week that I talked myself into leaving the room for more than just a shower or bathroom break, having regained enough control of myself to feel more at ease on the wheelchair. The staff didn't seem to mind, despite having me as a roadblock in the corridor at times.

The building's ground floor was like a narrow rectangle, with rooms on either side of a long corridor that spanned the length. Most of them were patient rooms, about another three multi-rooms and the rest single occupants.

The side that I was on had all the men, and the other side had the women.

No matter how many times I went back and forth along that corridor, peering into the open rooms at people at various stages of my condition, I couldn't see anyone close to my own age. The closest was Rich, whom I'm guessing was in his fifties to my thirty, the rest were all over sixty at the youngest.

It was another harsh reminder that I didn't really belong there.

One of the things that also slowly and subtly erodes you is

the lack of change in temperature. It was hospital heat level, and in some cases I can understand how this can make being stuck in the same place worse. You don't realise that the lack of stimulus sensation is like being slowly suffocated, like boiling a frog slowly.

I never left the building though, but I did hover near the entrance a few times. Just closed my eyes and felt the cold breeze, allowing myself to breathe the fresh air and calm down. Part of me wondered if I made it outside, would I be tempted to leave and head for home? It was close enough, even for someone in a wheelchair. There was a wide field between us, however, that the wheelchair would likely have got stuck in, so I'd have had to go around it. I wonder how far I would have got before they chased me down? Maybe halfway I'm guessing.

I never chanced it; a scolding was all that would await me, and a lot of my things were there too that I didn't like the idea of just leaving behind.

A few friends of my parents even sent me a fruit box: yep, you heard right, not a basket, a cardboard box full, like the sort that you get delivered to a work office once a week. Nothing exciting, just pears, apples, bananas, grapes, a few kiwis and a pineapple.

I have no idea how they expected me to be able to do anything but stare at the pineapple in a defeated way. Even my level of creativity couldn't help with that one, and I challenge anyone to try.

Fortunately, my dad cut it up and sent it back inside, making it possible for me to eat, instead of just making for an exotic paperweight.

The grapes were purple, and I found them sweeter than

I thought, probably the result of surviving on so much hospital food with a lot less artificial sugar.

There was a new therapy option too: breakfast prep!

I gather you get this one when they are considering letting you out, sort of like a controlled preview of how you'll do.

They had a small kitchen there and a nurse would watch as you went about getting some simple things put together. Things like safe kettle usage, toasting and buttering some bread, some cereal maybe depending on what you normally took. It was supposed to be as close to what you normally had at home and it was to check that you would be okay in practice.

I'm pleased to say that it didn't give me much trouble, and you got to eat what you made in the end. Despite being forced to just use my left hand for things like spreading butter, I took it slowly and breathed through the frustration when it hit me.

There's no greater motivation for success than need.

# Chapter 10

I don't know exactly what came over me, but I felt like I was filled with more energy than usual.

Maybe it was the physical proof that I could still perform tasks with only my left hand, finding ways to compensate for my lack of two hands, like using my mouth to hold things when needed.

Doing so I found made tying my shoe laces in the morning when I got dressed much easier. Ever tried to tie them one handed? I dare you to figure out a better way and not want to throw your shoe out the window. Using Velcro is cheating.

As the days passed by, I realised that I was getting quicker and quicker at getting dressed. Socks were still the most troublesome, but I was able to get them on after a minute or two after some initial practice. When I first got there, getting my clothes on was more of a chore, but I kept up with it, getting better at it and quicker.

It was proof I was getting better.

That, or I was just adapting to the situation over time.

I liked to keep myself clean too, even liked to keep a nail clipper around to keep my nails short. I had one with me on my car's keychain, but it was small and light, I think I got it out of a Xmas cracker.

Doing one hand wasn't too hard (my right), but the

problem came when I needed to do the other.

Spotted the problem yet?

I had trouble gripping it and applying force to the ends without dropping it with my right hand, yet I went slow and prayed that I didn't accidentally clip off the ends of one of my fingers. I knew when to give up though, when I couldn't reliably keep it gripped without potentially injuring myself.

The solution came about when I looked into my bathroom kit, which had a bigger one inside the bag. It had more surface area to grip and was easier to hold, with more angular sides to grip. It was still a chore, but I was able to persevere and finish both hands, mostly by using my palm and thumb. I didn't even entertain the notion of doing my feet, that was awkward enough back before the stroke, and no way was I going to take any unnecessary chances.

My face was also scraggly, with hair growth of over a few weeks. I had luckily shaved the weekend before my stroke, but it was way past due that I gave myself a fresher look. You just feel better brushing your hand over your bare chin and not feeling any bristles, only smooth skin.

Our bathroom also had a sink area with a mirror to the side as you went in, right before the toilet cubicle, which I only realised then.

Remember when I said I hadn't seen my face in ages due to a lack of reflective surfaces or mirrors?

I hadn't seen my face in almost a month now, and was still worried about seeing one side of it possibly slacker than the other, which I gather was the real reason for the absence of any mirrors around – it might upset the patients. It was possible for me to take a photo with my phone and look at it, but until then I just hadn't wanted to see myself.

My attempt at a beard wasn't thick – fortunately – nor was it too long so I didn't need to use scissors to trim it first. I was used to showering first, however, to soften the hairs and make it easier to cut, but I couldn't do that here. I used warm water to wet my face instead, giving it a minute or two before I started.

I always preferred to use the wet shave option, with foam instead of gel. The electronic shaver tended to tug too hard and sting my face for a second, and the former just seemed like a much cleaner method to use. I wasn't in the habit of shaving daily – more like weekly – so this was just the simplest choice for me.

When I saw myself in the mirror when I was done, it wasn't as bad as I thought. I didn't focus too much on anything other than what I was doing, so the beard got the most attention rather than the whole facial image. Since I was forced to use my left hand, I did end up cutting myself once or twice. Nothing too serious though, just a mild sting when the foam or water went across it. One of them was right over my lip too, so that one stung for a day or two till it scabbed and healed.

It took me almost an hour in there, with a new razor too. Before, I could do it in less than five minutes, but I didn't dwell on that, as this wasn't a race. No one seemed to need the toilet in the interim, and when I came out all freshly shaven, I honestly felt more like myself, like things were a little brighter now that I knew that there was something else that I could still do.

I was a lot more inquisitive on my travels too; I'd read the notice boards and posters along the walls for a bit of variety and distraction. They didn't change all that much, there was maybe a new A4 notice up once a week, so not that much variety over time.

There was one time 'T' was meant to be taken away for some relaxation therapy, but he asked if it was okay to stay in our room so the rest of us could join in. We all didn't mind either, as it was something different to do.

It involved listening to a CD, some kind of soothing meditative guide to finding somewhere calm in your mindscape, and allowing a tree to grow there from a seed. I didn't feel any different afterwards, but the voice was calming and it was a one-off moment where we got to spend an hour doing something different from staring at the walls or TV.

My calm place was a desert in my mind, somewhere I figured was quiet and out of the way. Most people believe that it's devoid of life, but I know that isn't true. You just have to stay still and pay attention.

I wouldn't have minded if we had more of those, but in the end it only happened once. I don't know if they continued it after I left, but I hope they did, as it was something different that I thought the other patients would enjoy.

After I had been there for almost two weeks, 'T' was ready to leave. He'd progressed from being stuck in his wheelchair to being able to steadily walk about with a stick to keep steady. His problem though, was his lack of feeling or sensation. I think it was coming back, but much slower than his control, so he needed to take things easy and be careful. He'd been going to the mini gym at the back of the physiotherapy area with more and more regularity, to the point he had to be told to calm down by the nurses.

I was sad to see him go and wished him well. We had agreed to have a drink or meal out after we all got out, so maybe I'd see him again, so it didn't feel like one of those absolute goodbyes that I hate. He was the resilient type, the kind that always remained cheery, calm and amiable, and from his progress, I knew he'd end up getting better in no time.

One of the nurses said that they could tell if a person would get better over time, that if one had the attitude to improve and get up then it was something they saw in them. 'T' was one of them and we all wished him a speedy recovery as he left.

I wondered if his family – a wife and one adult daughter that I knew of – would use this as an excuse to push him to retire from whatever he did. From the number of times he was on his laptop at the end, or in the gym, I silently wished them good luck with that with a light smile.

Then it was just Rich, George and me in the room, with one blank space at the back corner.

The nurses called George their troublemaker, which always elicited a smile from him. His foot bandages would itch throughout the day, and he'd wrestle with some kind of temporary boot to try and take it off every now and then. You have no idea how creative and patient an old person in a wheelchair with bandaged legs can be; given enough time I'm sure he would've managed to strip himself somehow if the nurses hadn't kept an eye on him.

So glad they did.

I gather that his feet weren't getting much better. Think

the reason he kept trying to take the bandages off was because they itched and stung, and I gather at some point that they'd become infected. The bits of his feet that I could see at times were red raw and inflamed, and didn't seem to be getting better over the time I was there.

Rich made me laugh by saying what they all got up to on Xmas here, how the nurses woke them up early and they all wore elf and Santa costumes with some Rudolf antlers. He joked that they'd almost tried an escape attempt involving a wheelchair chariot race, reminding me of some kind of Ben-Hur moment.

Apparently, the doctors said no. Bunch of buzzkills.

There was also some kind of electronic crane with a harness that they used to lift George out of his bed and into the chair. Well, it was the spare to that since there was something wrong with it. Rich also joked that they'd had the idea to use that to swing him clear out of the window to freedom when no one was looking, disregarding the injuries the glass shards would cause anyway.

The whole moment reminded me of *The Great Escape*, which cheered me up for a bit, before I realised, we were more like *One Flew Over the Cuckoo's Nest*, minus Nurse Ratched.

# Chapter 11

It wasn't long before I realised how lucky I had been with my roommates initially.

It was late in the evening when the open space in our room was filled, after nine p.m so we'd already tucked in for the night and got into bed with the lights off after taking our medication. My curtain was closed, but I could still hear what was going on around me easily, and the shadows silhouetted through the fabric also gave me some clue as to the events.

The gentleman's name (and I very loosely use the term) was Alexander. Don't think I ever learned his surname, nor did I want to after that night.

I'm guessing he was in his late seventies or eighties, but I can't confirm it.

They must've wheeled him in on a mobile bed as the space was minus one when I had last seen it, but I could make out what they were saying though not what they were doing past the curtains all that clearly since it was further away from me.

It seemed as if the place that had this man previously had transferred him last minute to this department and building, although neither myself nor the staff there had any notion of the 'hot medical potato' we'd just been tossed until he was already in the patient bubble.

His voice was annoyingly clear with a deep baritone,

and he never stopped talking. Well, more like complaining about how much pain he was in.

Not sure if he was on any medication but he kept hurling verbal abuse at the staff. Not swearing or anything, but just being unpleasant and loud, seeming to not care that this was a multi-room with other patients trying to sleep. I wonder if he ever actually knew that, or was just wrapped up in his own issues.

His complaints were interspersed with his pleas for someone to kill him; I gather the pain for him was pretty bad then, but did he really have to be so loud and clear? At first, a nurse was sitting next to him for observation, from the much quieter extra voice I heard, but she must have got tired of the abuse so left not long later with the door closing behind her.

But that didn't stop dear Alexander from ranting, and unlike her, I couldn't just leave the room to get away from him, although if I was sure I wouldn't be recaptured quickly thanks to the nurse's station right outside our room, I'd have considered crawling one-armed.

I have no idea how long we had to endure his endless whining, my voice was still messed up and I knew if I said anything out loud, he'd just drag me into his nonsense. I heard George respond a few times – in a rare moment of verbal clarity – for Alexander to shut up, so it wasn't just me getting annoyed.

I didn't hear a word from Rich though, but in the morning, I do recall seeing a pillow over his head as he slept on past our waking time, so he must've used it to drown out the sounds. Either that, or he could sleep through anything and had unusual sleeping habits.

Much like I guessed, George's comment didn't shut Alexander up at all, just gave him something to respond to. Again, I'll admit that he never said anything really nasty, it was more the selfish ranting, irrespective of others trying to sleep that wore away at you.

It went on for a while, and at some point, I think the nurses realised he wasn't going to stop anytime soon if they just left him alone. They wheeled out the entire bed into the hall, and I don't think he stopped complaining once. I was amazed that he was able to talk for so long and not get tired, which at this point felt like over an hour of non-stop talking.

Sadly, I don't think they moved him that far away, as even though they'd closed the room doors, I could still lightly make him out in the nightly silence. His voice didn't seem to be affected at all by the stroke he had, and he still kept going on and on, until at some point I managed to fall asleep I gather, which blissfully ended the suffering.

At some point, they put him and his bed back in the room, but nothing woke me up, showing just how tired I must have been at the time. He was in the previously empty spot when the curtains were pulled back, giving us our first glimpse at our nightly tormenter.

Like me, it looked as if his right side was the affected one, and I wondered if that had any bearing on our room position, or if it was just random.

He looked alert in the morning, despite the little sleep I'm guessing he had last night. It was also blessedly quiet, I also realised eventually, free of his sonorous ranting and wishes for someone to kill him. Whatever pain he was in had been temporary I suppose.

His face matched the voice, I would say, a slightly less than average height old man, with an overall tired and downcast feeling. I didn't need a nurse to tell me that he wasn't one of the positive ones who'd get better with time. Ironically, one still did, not long later, checking that I was all right after what she gathered had been a rather sleepless and unusual night from the night staff.

I think he had a wife back at home he mentioned once or twice; lucky her that he was now here to annoy us.

It was clear at breakfast time, after we'd all got up, that an apology wasn't coming, showing that he didn't appreciate how much of a pain to everyone he had been the previous night, nor did he care; if he even remembered in the first place.

This wasn't like a hotel, but he seemed to think he could say what he usually had at home and it would just magically be available here. Regardless of my unkind thoughts, I resolved not to get vocally involved with him and just hoped that by ignoring him he would get the message. He'd already soured the mood of the room by being there, and things felt notably more depressing and quieter afterwards.

Not that he seemed to be aware, it seemed.

There was no more ranting to everyone in the vicinity, but he didn't waste a moment to act the tired old man when a nurse did her usual rounds to check on us. I think he must've called for assistance into the toilet three or four times in less than an hour, without anything to show for it from what he said as he exited. He kept saying that he had to go, yet his body didn't seem to be on the same wavelength.

It was a weekday and Alexander had physio in the

afternoon, or at least it was planned for him. He didn't miss the chance to ask to go to the toilet first, and ended up doing little more than wasting everyone's time. When he came out, that was when he started to loudly complain. Nothing as bad as the previous night, but they were already now over thirty minutes into what should have been an hour-long session by then, without even getting him out the door, so he ended up not going due to lack of leftover time.

There was also a medical cream he had in his bathroom kit, that he kept trying to get the nurses to apply to his legs, something about them being sore and cramping and that he normally had this done daily. I don't know why he couldn't do this himself, and the more I saw him complaining the more I realised that he'd all but given up.

No one said anything to him, and the general camaraderie that there seemed to be had all but vanished in his presence. From the words I heard at the nurses' station, he'd been passed around a few places for his disruptive nature, and it was only after they had accepted him that they all realised what they'd been landed with, and now couldn't return. Who knows if they managed to pass him onto somewhere else after I left, but if not I'll wager that they gave him his own solitary room and kept the doors closed when they could.

Let that be a lesson to you: never accept a last-minute delivery if something feels off, especially if it's sentient.

That night seemed to be a calm one for him thankfully, as we didn't get a repeat of his previous night, which was something I'd been dreading all day long. If it did happen, all I could hope for was that I was tired enough to fall asleep fast.

# Chapter 12

I myself was doing a lot better now. I had advanced enough with my leg physio that they had given me a walking stick to use, but still told me to be careful and take it easy. I thought this would free me from the need to ask for help to the toilet, but no such luck; I still needed an escort for my walk of shame. I found that out after a scolding one time I came back out, after going on my own.

It was the annoying scolding kind too, the one that guilted you. I wouldn't have really cared if it was just on me, but the nurse said that they would get in trouble if I kept doing that, so I was guilt tripped into being compliant since I didn't want them to get into trouble for something I had done.

I never had a chance to take a trip around the buildings outside on my feet, as the consultant in charge of me appeared to say I would be leaving today.

Now, considering how badly I wanted to leave when I first got there, this didn't give me as much of a feeling of excitement as I thought it would. I'd got used to being there, had created a routine for myself and everything, although part of me was glad to get out now that 'Alexander' had been added to the room.

I was excited for the rest of the day, since my pickup time by my parents was later in the afternoon – I was all packed and ready to go by mid-morning, showing how eager I was.

In terms of time, I'd been indoors for about two and a half weeks, minus the trip to the new specialist building after a week, which meant I hadn't gone outside on my own feet in almost a month.

I really wanted to see our family dog again, I just felt better stroking her and just seeing her through the window before was hard. Sasha was her name, and she really didn't like being held, although she did love the belly rubs.

Time soon passed, and I was all set to leave, just like 'T' before me. As I passed Rich for the last time, I wanted to give him my phone number on a piece of paper, for that meal we all promised to have together after a while when we'd all got better. He brushed it off though, and said he'd just get it from the nurses later. I wasn't sure this was allowed, but he said it would be okay and waved me goodbye. I wasn't sure if George would make it out, but I knew Rich would, albeit his recovery seemed slower than mine.

George too mumbled a goodbye, I think. I didn't care about Alexander, I think he realised too that all of us just tolerated his annoying presence, but he still said goodbye too, and I hoped he wouldn't cause too many more problems for the other patients or the nurses.

My large box of fruit was almost empty, but I still had a few things left. I ended up leaving it behind for the staff, along with a few other snacks as a thank you for everything they'd all done. You weren't really allowed to bring in much due to the bubble, so I made do with what I had there at the time as opposed to trying to bring anything in.

I hoped that lockdown restrictions and COVID would

be over soon, allowing me to go back and thank them properly, with a card maybe, steady on my feet this time to dispel the image of me in a wheelchair or with a walking stick.

I had a new wheelchair ordered for me too, to use at home, but I used my walking stick to walk out, taking in a breath of cold air due to leaving on my own after what seemed like forever.

I wanted to cry a little when I got out to my parents' car, slowly easing myself in and not rushing like I wanted. It would be just my luck that I would have somehow injured myself just as I was leaving hospital, and the last thing I wanted was to be dragged back inside for another month.

My parents had parked next to the main door, so I didn't have far to walk in the end. Although I was walking again, I didn't have the stamina to stay up for long, so I was advised to do it in short bursts for now.

I was going to be staying with my parents for the time being, so they took me back to their place, which wasn't far away, just about five minutes' drive.

When I got back, I made my way slowly to my usual spot on the sofa, dropping down with a sigh and realising that so much had happened since I last sat there. Our dog was there too, and she was ready to demand her usual belly rub, lying on her back and raising her paw as if to tell me to stroke more and more, eventually setting her head down when my pace was just right, though how she left the leg up when she fell asleep, I'll never know.

I couldn't help but laugh at her usual attitude that I'd missed.

Apart from the wheelchair, there were a few other pieces of kit we were given. One of them was a plastic stool for the shower cubicle, which would allow me to sit steadily, instead of leaning against the wall whilst standing on wet marble. I never ended up using it as it was intended, it was put to use as a bedside table in the end, as I wanted to push myself to learn how to keep my balance quicker.

Another thing was a free-standing set of bars around the toilet set on a frame that overlapped the bowl, which made it easier to set myself down and vice-versa. I think there was also some kind of specialised toilet seat, but I never used that while I was there.

A few of the things I didn't want any more was to have soup, or to watch BBC One on television. The former had been a daily staple during lunch, and now it made me feel like an invalid, whereas the latter had become intolerably boring having to watch it all day long in the multi-patient room. During the evening it was okay, but the day was filled with endless local news (most of it bad) and antique or bargain shows; the idea of being glued to a TV set watching these made me feel older than I was.

I didn't want to be a bother, so normally just stayed in my sofa spot, reading my web novels quietly, or listening to some music. I'm kind of all over the place with what I like, but if I like it, I like it. I think I listened to a lot of *Skillet* though, and some modern Country if it was upbeat enough. It occurred to me then that having the radio on within the hospital ward would have been a nice alternative to the TV.

You can lose yourself in a good song, regardless of your physical condition, and it can lift your spirits even if you aren't feeling so great.

My parents were pottering about the house and usually left me to my own devices, but they gave me control of the TV, which I didn't use that often really. Normally I would just have something on in the background, an old British sitcom usually to make me laugh. One of the few things that my dad and I liked to watch was *Only Fools and Horses*, or *Dad's Army*, so it was normally something along those lines. It became a bit of a game, as I was trying to keep myself from laughing out loud a lot, something that I had been doing since my stroke – along with getting too emotional in general.

I tried to keep my same toilet schedule, as pedantic as it sounds, seeing as how it had worked well for me in hospital. The bathroom was on the first floor, which meant I had a flight of stairs to climb, but I was able to do it one step at a time as I'd been shown. Going up and down stairs on my own had been covered in later physio sessions, so I knew to take it slow and lead with my good leg, one step at a time before moving onto the next. At first, I was advised to have someone keep an eye on me as I climbed, but after a week I felt confident enough to do it unwatched.

It felt freeing being able to go to the toilet myself, without needing to ask someone for help, as if I had taken back something important to me. No longer would I have to announce it by pressing a button for the entire nurses' station to know that I was needing to go again, possibly for a bowel movement.

Due to my recent hospital stay, I also now appreciated the importance of staying hydrated. I think before, I was only getting just over half the average recommended amount per day for an adult, minus food intake. I had a lot of headaches before, but not so much now that I was drinking more, so I didn't want to go back to that. No more would I be forced to carry around a pack of aspirin at times.

Eating normal food was another challenge for me. I had got used to eating with just my left hand over time; the trickiest thing being rice, but now I had to figure out a way to eat something new – spaghetti pasta.

I couldn't use a spoon with my other hand to twirl it in, so I had to use the base of the plate, which was a lot less controlled than what I was used to. It took me a bit longer, but when you're hungry you don't give up easily on food, eventually finishing the full plate without using my hands or making a mess. God forbid that I made myself look like some kind of barbarian that ate with his bare hand.

Well, at least on that occasion it went okay. I remember that one time I set my tray on the coffee table, but hadn't balanced it properly in time, letting my plate full of red sauce pasta hit the light grey carpet. I don't think it helped that the hot plate slid more easily along the smooth plastic base of the tray.

I felt bad, but it cleaned up without a problem, but I hated to waste food like that, and never made a similar mistake like that again. To be fair, it's amazing what a few sprays of watered-down Dettol can help you wipe off, without leaving any trace.

To make it easier to balance my tray, I even got something to drink and carried it through separately, a new habit I seem to have made after the entire experience that I've kept up even over a year on now.

# Chapter 13

It was around mid-week when I was discharged from the hospital stroke unit, so I had the rest of the week and weekend free. I was to be given supported discharge over the course of the following six weeks at home, where a nurse or two would come round to go over a few exercises with me, about three times a week.

When I left the hospital, they had asked if I still wanted to continue with my speech therapy, but I'm not really one for talking and am quite introverted by nature, and my voice had got much better by then and I could say more than a few simple words without repeating myself to get my point across, so I said thank you, but no.

It was unusual sleeping in a room again by myself, and the bed was much softer and comfier than in the hospital. I still maintained my nine p.m bed time – still trying to continue the routine – of course I woke up early the next morning around six a.m. I'd just lie there, trying to force myself back to sleep, with minimal success, until around eight a.m, which I thought was a more respectable time to get up.

Now that I had some privacy, I also tried to do some self-exercising. Nothing too big, just some push-ups: I couldn't even do one. My right side was still too weak to support my body weight, even when using my knees as pivot points rather than my feet to reduce the weight I pushed up. Clearly, I still wasn't back to normal, despite my change in surroundings being more familiar to me.

There was a sense of freedom then, like I could get up whenever I wanted, could shower when I wanted, could eat whenever, and could even go to bed when I chose to. You don't realise how this lack of free will eats at you, not until you lose it. Anyone who has been in hospital will understand the feeling, the reliance you feel on others for even the most basic thing.

For someone more independent and older, they'd eventually be driven mad by such a need and I was once again glad to be home.

I went out with my dad too on walks once a day, nothing too long just around the block, short bursts I remembered I'd been advised repeatedly. Even that tired me out, and my hip hurt if I pushed myself and went too far or too fast. I later realised that when you walk your hips rotate too, that there's muscle movement further up rather than just in the legs. I'm guessing that my muscles still weren't strong enough to stay tense, so my leg bone joint was more harshly grating against my hip bone, leading to the pain. It became less and less over time and allowed me to go further for longer, but I certainly felt the effects.

It's not like I had a lack of energy, I recovered that pretty quick and didn't resort to daily napping at all, nor did I feel that tired in general. Just out of breath and winded really if I exerted myself, but nothing serious.

The following week, I had my first visit from one of the appointed nurses. I couldn't believe the amount of time she needed to spend putting on PPE as she arrived, and she had to do that with a new set every time she visited someone. All of it was thrown away too afterwards, and I shuddered to think of how much disposable income she was running through. It was all paid for the by the NHS, but still, it seemed like an utter waste.

We were still in the pandemic then in early February of 2021, so the contact between households was strict. I got a few cards from some friends and relatives, but never really saw anyone in the six-week period back, apart from the hazmat-wearing nurses. It wasn't that really, but the get up was close enough that you felt like a quarantine patient: gloves, apron, mask, visor etc.

Much like back at the hospital it was leg physio with some core work too, giving me a tailored list of exercises to perform on my own if I wanted to speed things up. I really, really did by that point.

By then, I could more or less walk unsteadily without relying on the stick, so I had stopped using it. Same for the custom wheelchair I'd been given, don't think I ever unwrapped that or even sat in it, sadly. Hopefully it ended up being used by someone who really needed it after it got sent back.

For the session I had my shirt off and jeans rolled up, allowing her to see the muscle movements in my body to confirm that I was moving in the correct way. I once commented on wanting to get better fast, and she asked me if I wanted to walk faster or properly. As much as I wanted to say the former, the latter was what I silently knew was the correct answer to the rhetorical question.

Unlike the one push-up I'd tried – and failed badly –

these exercises I could do as they were much easier and focused on one muscle at a time, so I kept up with them once a day while judging myself as I progressed. There was more than one session of physio per week, around two at different points days apart, but the other I would say was more for dexterity.

A different nurse would arrive, getting wrapped up like a Xmas present with gloves and a mask, with a few simple aids. It was a Tupperware box with some things inside, some pegs, small cones, dominoes and loose change etc.

The idea was to set them up, or pick them up with my right hand. She also gave me a handwriting booklet to try out, the kind kids get in school when they're starting out writing joined words to practice.

At that point I realised that I hadn't tried writing anything yet.

Not that I could, being right-handed and all, but I suddenly wanted to see what it looked like now.

The verdict: less than good. I think calling it chicken-scratch would have been a compliment.

Although you could see the letters, my control of the pen was shaky and the letters came out wiggly and misshapen. I didn't do much, just tried to write out the alphabet and single digit numbers to see, really not liking the results. I still have the notebook I used, so I can look back and see exactly how bad it was compared to later. I used it once a day for a week or two and I could see from the style that it was getting better with time and practice.

Still, this was better than not being able to write at all.

True, in society, we now mostly use keyboards or phones to type – instead of doing it by hand, which seems to be getting slowly passed out – but there's something unique about being able to write yourself. Typing is bland and reveals nothing about the person, whereas handwriting shows so much more. It's almost like an art in itself, and even has one: calligraphy. Some writing I've seen looks amazing, nothing complex or poetic, just simple text. It's mostly women who write like that, so I wasn't likely to reach that level.

I also took some small pride in the fact that my own writing was better and more legible than my two younger brothers' squiggle like words, a card or two showing recent examples nearby for all to see.

Pen and paper also can't be hacked like a computer file, not that I was really paranoid or anything – nor had anything bad happen to me like that – I just preferred having the privacy and security.

The dexterity nurse also asked if I had any simple hobbies we could use as an exorcise, which I actually did. I'm not quite sure if she expected me to respond that way.

I'd always liked doing hand-crafts, and usually try a range of things when the mood strikes me. One of the things I did regularly was model miniatures; small plastic models you have to build from a kit and paint. Putting them together was considered tricky at times depending on the kit, and required delicate control of the hands, so she was fine with monitoring me doing a few of those.

Apart from that there was another round of breakfast preparation. Nothing major, just simple things in the end, not a full course meal. Things like toast again and cups of tea, showing that I was able to do that in my own environment without any problems or spilling anything. I think I may have ended up making a breakfast bun one week, but some of that had already been cooked by my parents and I just had to heat it up and assemble things to my liking.

I was getting more movement back in my hand by now, only the fingers were still giving me trouble, but I could use my arm more easily now than before.

Still, I didn't push it, not with knives and hot water around. I resorted to using my left for most things, showing that I had adapted to my situation and didn't take any risks that would end up with me back in hospital.

The nurse had to correct me a few times, wanting to see the progress in my right hand more than judging how I was coping. I was getting better so fast that I needed to regain the feel of using both hands again now for everything instead of compensating with my left, trying until I was annoyed and then resorting to it for ease and speed.

# Chapter 14

The timetable was flexible and differed every week, with most of the times being set closer to the end of the week, over the phone at times, sometimes involving a cancellation and change if needed.

I was getting along well, without anything accidental happening, except for the pasta incident but that was more of an injury to the carpet.

There was one moment though that I realise now was dumb, yet at the time I thought I could handle it and invariably thought it would be a good idea.

I'll give you a quick preview: it wasn't.

For the model miniatures I was doing, you needed to use a specific type of glue to bond things together (not including your fingers), and I didn't like the idea of ordering online and having to wait a week even if it was cheaper. Luckily for me, I had a few friends who shared the hobby that lived nearby, and one of them had a spare pot of glue.

See where I'm going with this yet?

Oh, he only lived about twenty minutes' walk away too, so I thought that was perfect: a nice little walk to see how I was progressing, whilst also doing a useful errand.

What I had failed to consider at the time, or to be honest just brushed aside in my mind as a 'minor detail', was that this was power walking speed. Or that there was still lingering snow and ice outside from winter that made walking on the pavement more precarious even for someone with full function, let alone me.

Oh, also it was at night, after my parents had gone to bed early so I'd be going alone, without anyone's knowledge.

Yep, those were just some 'minor details'.

It wasn't too bad getting there, although the slushy snow was annoying to wade through, often walking much slower and hoping I didn't step on a hidden patch of ice.

I tried to walk mainly on the smoother roads but still slipped a little due to the compactness of the snow and spots of glassy ice where water had pooled and frozen.

Still, it was quicker than trudging through crunchy snow, albeit less stable for my footing.

On the plus side I never fell over, despite the few amounts of close calls. I didn't take my walking stick; I didn't want to rely on it too much and using it made me feel worse. Admittedly I also didn't want to be seen outside needing a stick to help me walk.

The only thing was that it took me twice the amount of time to get there, which meant I had more time in the cold, but I still made it and took it as a personal triumph. It was nice to see my friend in person too. Ironically enough, his mom was recently admitted to the main hospital, so he knew all about the restrictiveness the NHS was currently working under.

I hadn't seen any of my friends in all that time since I first got ill, so it was kind of like a nostalgic feeling. Even before then I hadn't seen much of them as we were in the middle of a lockdown that had gone on for months.

I got some spare glue and hoped she would be okay, realising that under lockdown measures and my own condition that the odds of visiting were non-existent. I didn't go in, didn't want to breach guidance measures and shortly after, we said our goodbyes after catching up a little.

Now it was time for the long and cold walk home.

Remember when I said I was told to walk in short bursts?

I'd been on my feet walking now for almost an hour, and really wished I had followed that advice, feeling the pain in my right hip again with more of a vengeance with every step. On my way back, it got so bad that I had to lift my leg up with my hands pulling up my jeans, forcing myself to walk through the pain.

No one knew I was out there, and calling my parents for a lift would have woken them up. I also felt like that would've been like giving up on me somehow. I was here because of my own choice, however ill advised, and it was up to me alone to get back. I could have called for a taxi or UBER, but again that felt like giving up.

If I wanted then I could have even just collapsed and waited for someone to help and call an ambulance.

Who cared that I was in pain, so what that I was alone?

I was responsible for me, no one else, and I'd grown used to needing that feeling of control. I needed to get it back, even if it came with a little pain.

If you wanted to move, then move. Otherwise, there wasn't really much point to anything.

I'd got a glimpse of what it was like stuck to a bed; a prisoner in my own body. Maybe that hell was what was waiting for me eventually, but not now and not today.

The return trip took even longer, and by the time I dragged myself back into my own street, I sighed with relief as I knew it would soon be over. The whole misadventure had taken about two hours, something that I had expected to have taken under half the time, yet clearly I had overestimated my recovery speed.

I made it home and into bed shortly after, not taking long to fall asleep and leaving my parents none the wiser to my long nightly walk.

As you can guess, come the next morning, I really felt it in my hip. Not so much when I was motionless, but putting weight on it really hurt but not enough to preclude me from doing anything, otherwise I'd never been able to leave the bed.

To make matters worse, I had a leg physio appointment that day in a few hours, and I hoped it would be gone by then.

No such luck though, I even had to admit to the nurse what I had done, as doing the exercises was too painful for me. I couldn't quite tell what her expression was behind that mask, but I guessed it wasn't too kind.

She understood that I wanted to get better quickly, but urged that I should take things more slowly, lest I take a step backwards during my recovery process.

She modified the exercises to take my pain into account, hoping that in a few days no permanent damage would have been done. I learned my lesson, having been slightly guilted into accepting it, though mostly it was the sharp pain whenever I put pressure on my hip.

# Chapter 15

Fortunately for me, the pain didn't persist for too long. Only for a few days afterwards, so no lasting harm was done. I chose to see it as a step backwards, since it could have easily gone the other way, and it would have been entirely my fault for being impatient and pushing myself too soon.

At this point, it had been almost two months since the whole event had started, and I was feeling the lack of variety.

It felt like I was in a cage inside another cage, as the UK lockdown due to COVID still persisted, with the daily news still reporting nearly the exact same thing every day. What it all amounted to, and what everyone was saying was that it would be over when it was over.

The idea of 'returning to normality' became meaningless, as this had now become the new normal.

Much like in the hospital, I didn't get any visitors at home. I'm guessing they felt that standing outside the front door and only being seen through the window was a waste of time, not to mention that it was still winter conditions outside for us. My parents probably also told them not to come, since they knew I liked my privacy.

The snow and ice were gradually melting, but it was a slow process and the icy conditions persisted as a result.

I spent most of my time in the living room, reading or playing an app game on my tablet computer.

There was a working TV in my room, but I didn't like the idea of shutting myself away like that and felt that it would be too easy to wallow in self-pity.

My dad was the active type and had recently retired, so seemed to be trying to keep himself busy. The garden was his current project – nothing major or obsessive seeming – just a variety of plant pots set up, big and small.

We had a big conservatory, so he didn't need to use a greenhouse, not that we could have fit one in. Well, we could, but there would have been too little room for the plants since there were already three sheds. Or more like two and a moped safe storage shed-like thing, which obviously wasn't used to store the moped in the end. He was currently on model number two, since the first had been stolen one night a few years back, right out of the 'safe storage' shed, funny enough.

He made a police report, but it wasn't likely he'd get the thing back as we found pieces of the body down in the local field/park area a few minutes away, telling us it had already been stripped.

So, I guess his paranoia with its storing inside the house was warranted.

He never used it anyway since he retired and mainly used it to get to his work depot and back.

It almost cost him a few fingers in the end.

Behind where we live is a long and narrow lane, which connects to our back garden. Every morning my dad would drive his moped out of it, which at first wasn't a problem. This was a while back – a few years now – and I think it happened near winter. As a result, he was wrapped up well, with thick gloves and a hat.

Thankfully, he wore the thick gloves.

One morning, whilst driving out of the back lane, he

ended up taking the exit too tightly, and scraped his two little-most fingers of his right hand against the wall. It wasn't a normal wall either; it was clad with small white stone chips. The effect was like grating cheese.

I was at work at the time, so I got all this third hand from my mom at the hospital. It wasn't anything overly serious, she said, though I could imagine the scene being filled with blood as my dad traipsed back home, and her panicking for a moment or two.

I could hear an 'I told you so' tone in her voice, since she'd never really liked the idea of my dad getting one of those things at his age. She seemed to be mentioning his age more now, and how it wasn't a good thing that he stayed so active. Funny that she seems to have got more active now with long walks.

He needed surgery on his fingers – which he ended up getting on the same day. As a result he kept his fingers and I can't really see too much scarring from a distance, even now. He lost his two nails though, but I gather from his comments that he didn't mind so much as he kept the fingers.

Now that it's fully healed I don't think there's much issue with it, apart from the occasional pain that shoots through them whenever he bangs them against something. Of course he kept the moped, and continued to use it until he retired not long after, much to my mom's annoyance.

I think she was happy when it got stolen, but then he got another one and the happiness quickly faded away. He never uses it now; it just sits there in the conservatory as a reminder, albeit an unused one.

# Chapter 16

Aside from that, my dad liked to bake.

It wasn't like we watched TV baking shows really, just the occasional cooking program. There's something about watching food being cooked that makes you want to try what you see being made.

And then there was my mom.

She was only slightly less active than he was, though not so prone to serious injury. Accident prone yes, to the point where our dog could still sleep soundly through her kitchen yelps now.

The two of us watched a lot of TV crime dramas in the evening, even before the stroke, so we started that up again soon after I came home. What were we onto by then? We've watched a lot of things, but I think at that point we were watching the *NCIS* series, can't remember which one as there's so many to keep track of now.

She was in a 'work from home' situation, doing a lot of her work on her laptop up in my parents' room on her own. Other than that, she seemed to like to trawl through TV networks and streaming services for different dramas to watch in her spare time.

Not the procedural and episodic crime stuff that we watched together, but the other drama things that I found endlessly boring – especially the new British ones. There are far too many long silences and local landscape shots, like they're trying to subliminally sell the rural UK as a tourist spot.

That's how my days at home went by: my parents and I doing our own things, with the family dog as my usual company. She liked to have her belly rubbed, would lift her leg up in almost a regal way as if to silently demand it. I used my right hand, which was slowly starting to regain finer control, gently stroking her as a finger control exercise.

I had gained a sense of numbness in my fingers now that faded away as I regained control of them, similar to the pins and needles after-feeling. First to fade was my thumb, then index finger and middle. The only ones left were the two smallest. I'd already got the use of my arm back now, so only the fingers were left.

I'd kept up the daily walking around the block, just fifteen minutes at a time now on my own. I was walking fine now and getting closer to my former speed – I still couldn't move quickly up any stairs without losing my balance at the end, as my rhythm kept being thrown off and I felt unsteady, having to reach out to the wall to support myself.

In the fifth week, the nurse in charge of my physiotherapy asked if it would be okay to bring a nursing student with her to observe. I was a good patient, she said, and I was making such a fast recovery that she admitted she wished they'd recorded it at the start, just so I could see the difference with my current progress that she was seeing.

I barely recalled that I had seen something similar back at the hospital stroke ward in one of my earliest sessions: a nurse with a camera filming an older patient as they walked unsteadily.

Walking was no issue now for me, as long as I didn't go too fast or for too long. Actual movement on my feet had helped regain some of the muscle I had lost, I think, over the first month or so when I was unable to move my right side much. The lack of use of my right limbs had meant loss of some muscle, so I wanted to get moving again.

If I went slow and easy then I was fine, but if I tried to push it like running or going up the stairs quickly, then I'd lose my movement rhythm and have to stop.

At this point, it was the final week of my supported discharge.

Everything had gone great, mostly, and I found myself feeling sad at the idea of it all ending. Despite it being a terrible thing, it had been an experience – one where I got to meet and interact with many new people. Even if it was for something I didn't like or had dreaded, I never liked the ending.

In our last session, the physio nurse said she would refer me to a nearby rehabilitation centre for some additional treatment, which was more physio work essentially. It wasn't to a faraway place, the rehab centre was just opposite the road from the stroke ward I was in, about ten to fifteen minutes' walk away.

Horizons, it was called.

It was recently repaired, as not long ago some van or lorry had damaged the reception overhang at the entrance – which meant that patients had to come in from the rear entrance previously. It had all been finished now, and you couldn't really tell.

She put me down for another six weeks' referral, and I got accepted easily enough. It was for about an hour each week; I got to use the gym room that had about eight to ten machines. I don't know what they were called as I never got their names, but each one seemed to work on a particular set of muscles.

None of the equipment was electronic and it was all manual. One or two of them I never used, due to them needing fixing at the time with an 'out of order' sign over them.

I'd move around the room every five minutes or so to a different machine and being timed on each one, alternating working my legs and then my arms. It was your typical push and pull in most cases – nothing too complicated – and I didn't once feel short of energy or like I had overworked myself. I'm not a super fit or athletic person; I just didn't find any of it exhausting.

One week I ended up using a stationary bicycle (which actually was electronic), pushing the settings up as high as I could and just pedalling against the increased resistance. On another I was using the parallel bars to let them check my walking progress with safe support, probably to see that I hadn't picked up any bad habits. I hadn't, as it turned out, despite my one time badly planned nightly trip, so no lasting damage had been done as a result of that.

# Chapter 17

Around the period my referral to Horizons rehab centre started, I also ended up going back to work. Nothing major, just a few days a week to try and get back into the habit. I wasn't involved in any labour or physical job: it was in an office as a Technical Assistant – just basically admin work.

There had also been the process with the car insurance and DVLA, confirming to them that I didn't have any permanent disability as a result of the stroke, which had been confirmed by the nurse in charge of my physiotherapy. There wasn't any problem with that, just a phone call or two and some online forms filled out, with some being sent to me in the post to have the originals, I believe.

At the very least I don't think my annual insurance price went up by much, if at all.

When I arrived it felt strange.

The last time I had been here was about two and a half months ago, less than an hour before my stroke happened. I remarked to myself that so much could change when you least expected it to, all in but a moment.

I worked for a private Oil Engineering Consultancy & Management firm, in one of the old-style houses along one of the main roads towards the middle of the town centre. I was in an office on the first floor, so as you can guess: stairs.

I still couldn't climb them that fast; I had to take it slow and steady and I seemed to like having one hand on the nearest wall for additional lateral support, or whatever was close by and firm at the time. I still vividly recalled losing my balance as I went from the A&E waiting area to the nurse's room and didn't want a repeat of that no matter how small the possibility was.

There weren't many people in; we were still in a 'work from home' advised situation in March 2021, so office visits were sparse for all throughout the week. I had always maintained two days in the office a week, ever since the start, to give myself a sense that I still worked there, instead of getting too used to a laptop and forwarded calls.

I also think I was living the nearest to it at about five minutes' drive away, so it was easy for me compared to the others.

Of course, my streak had now been broken for all the time I had been away.

I was lucky that I hadn't lost my job, that I had an understanding boss that confirmed early on that my job would be safe and waiting for me when I was feeling better. I was anxious about that at first, but my dad had spoken to my boss and relayed this to me in the first or second week, I think, which helped take a weight off my mind at the time, looking back.

It was still COVID lockdown and losing my job at this point wouldn't have been good moneywise. I'm not sure how long it would have taken me to get another job at that point, when everyone seemed afraid to come close to each other without multiple sets of PPE equipped, and by close, I mean within two metres.

There weren't many people in the office when I started to come back in, about one or two others at most. It wasn't a large company anyway, but it was a far cry from what I remembered.

Those that I met were really nice about it all, and I enjoyed having more people to talk to, now that I sort of could. My speaking out loud had improved over time, and I could say things more clearly, less in a mumble sort of way. In my head it still sounded like I had a kind of an echo, but those I asked said that I sounded fine and they were able to understand me no issue.

That, or they were just being polite about it, considering what I'd gone through.

Things also seemed to be slowly getting back to normal for me at that point. Well, as normal as can be in these abnormal times. I'd stopped staying with my parents round about the same time I went back to work, so I was back to living alone. I still needed to take things slower, to not push myself, or else I would get tired out quickly.

Everything was finally starting to get back to normal, and I continued my rehab at the Horizons centre without problem, eventually finishing it about a month and a half later.

A few months later I went to a photo booth at my local supermarket, to get a new picture for my recently expired passport. I wasn't planning on going anywhere abroad, nor should I be considering my medical predicament.

I ended up redoing it over and over, eventually realising that the right side of my face looked slightly off around the mouth, even when I felt I had no expression. That side of my lip was uptilted a little and it was a depressing reminder of why I had never taken a selfie photo of myself to see how I looked, even though so much time had passed by at this point.

The really annoying thing is that I still look like that even over a year on from that, so it's unfortunately something I've got to live with. In the grand scheme of things, only having that and the medication I take daily as a reminder of the experience, I think I got off pretty lightly.

A more subtle reminder of the event is a slight weakness in my right side, both my hand and my leg. If I have 100% control of my left, I'd say I have around a 90% level of control on my right. It's not often an issue, and doesn't affect much really, though I recently discovered that I'm not so good at playing snooker any more, so any kind of fine control sport is out, not that I played any before fortunately.

It was… a humbling thing I feel. A sneak preview of where we're all going to end up, assuming we're all lucky enough to survive till old age, though I'm not sure 'lucky' is the right term to use after going through it. For me, I still have over half my life where I can do what I like without any real physical limitation, but for all of the others in the stroke ward, there wasn't this hopeful ending to look forward to. Some of them would be stuck with disabilities and further restrictions, making their remaining years potentially rather bleak.

This hopeful outlook I had for myself was one of the main reasons that I got better so quicky, being back to myself mostly after only three months. Thank God the stroke occurred when I was with my parents, or I'm not sure I would have made it to the hospital within the four-hour period, making it easier to reverse.

Where would I be now if I hadn't?

I'd like to think that I'd have got better regardless, just more slowly, but I truly can't be sure of that.

I used to be a lot more anxious about the future, to let worries about tomorrow or next week affect how I was today. Not so much any more. I mean I still keep the future in mind, but no longer am I willing to play the what-if game with a perpetually negative outcome. You don't realise how amazing it really is to just be able to walk unaided on your own, whenever you want, for whatever you want, until it's taken away from you.

For most people of a much older age that suffered this, being able to use a walking stick is the best to hope for, yet it was almost like a second chance for me, as the final destination was much further off.

So, here's to hoping that I don't have another any time soon, for at least another forty years or more, if ever. Despite how humbling it was, I really don't want to go through that again, though I now know that I'd be okay mentally. I think.

In the multi-room I was in, it was almost like seeing the various life stages of age.

First was Rich, just starting to reach his sixties, then was 'T' at the point where you are active and don't want to quietly get older, rebelling against the slow decline. Then there was George, who was more of a horror story with the level of care he needed.

I recently saw on the news that they're doing a stroke scenario with one of the main casts for a TV evening soap show. It felt a little ironic.

Those kinds of shows aren't something I watch, far too many bad things happening that makes it unbelievable, but

I guess it attracts more viewers somehow.

I can't help but think that they missed a trick.

Not just for a stroke, but any kind of serious condition that required a stay in hospital. We were out of lockdown now, but recovery during that time was… different.

You couldn't really have visitors easily, and the nurses had to wear all of that PPE, which dehumanised them, I think, as you couldn't see their facial expressions. Even the visitors you could have were limited to household family; I didn't see most of my friends till months later, so I felt even more alone.

There were other patients nearby you could speak to, but their recent experience was similar to your own, forced to stare at the blank walls most of the time, dealing with their own mental trauma regarding their current condition and how permanent it all was.

My age compared to all of the others also stood out to me, making me feel out of place.

# Epilogue

It's been over a year now, and I think I've recovered as much as I'm going to.

I've got full function back on my right side, well, more or less. Compared to my left side, I'd say that my right has about 90% of the speed, but there's still good control and sensation. It isn't really enough to make me notice, I just have to be careful not to go too fast or my left outpaces my right.

There's also a numb pins and needles like feeling that I sometimes get in my right hand. The autonomous reaction when I yawn or stretch, where my right side tries to extend on its own, still hasn't left and probably won't.

I feel like I'm overly complaining at this point, so many never recover so much and even less so quickly. If I had to stay in hospital for six months then I'm not sure how stir crazy I would have been at the end.

I'll freely admit it now; mentally, I don't believe it all affected me much. It worries me a little that I could be so detached for something so serious, for almost dying from a medical condition I had no clear warning about. Like I said, the experience was a humbling one for me.

Recalling scenes of George back at the stroke unit being extensively cared for, and his downcast demeanour, Rich getting emotional on the phone to his family, the other patients in the unit I could see during one of my wanderings as I pushed my wheelchair through the building.

I could have been so much worse, my luck just seemed to work with me this time, but maybe not the next. In the back of my mind, I'm always worried that I'll slowly get worse again, so I do some light exercises at night when I take my medication. If I can do them all, then I still have control, and I'm safe for another day.

Would I say that I'm different? I don't know.

Maybe I am in some small ways, yes, perhaps I'm still changing as I'm doing things now that I didn't much before. I don't really watch much live TV now, I prefer just to listen to some music, and I'm doing a little cooking – something I used to dislike. I also get a lot angrier now and am less tolerant of things I don't like, shaping things in more of a way that I want, instead of trying to please other people.

The anger I feel is towards myself, at my previous self anyway, for having accepted things like that. I use the feeling to push myself, doing small things that I normally wouldn't like forcing myself to clean my house fully. Something I hadn't done since I moved in six years ago.

I'm so thankful to all of the NHS nurses and hospital staff that helped me during my stay, and my family for supporting and caring for me afterwards. Without all of them, I don't know where I'd be.

Thank you all so much.